SOLAR POWER

A TRUE BOOK®

by

Christine Petersen

Children's Press®
A Division of Scholastic Inc.

New York Toronto London Auckland Sydney
Mexico City New Delhi Hong Kong
Danbury, Connecticut

The Sun shines brightly through the clouds.

Reading Consultant
Jeanne Clidas
*State University of
New York College*

Content Consultant
Tony Rogers
*Renewable Energy
Research Laboratory,
University of Massachusetts*

Library of Congress Cataloging-in-Publication Data

Petersen, Christine.
    Solar power / Christine Petersen.
        p. cm. — (A True book)
    Summary: Describes how the sun's energy supports all living things on Earth and how it is used as a power resource to create electricity.
    Includes bibliographical references and index.
    ISBN 0-516-22807-2 (lib. bdg)   0-516-21941-3 (pbk.)
    1. Solar energy—Juvenile literature.   [1. Solar energy.] I. Title.
II. Series.
TJ810.P425 2003
621.47—dc22

                                                                          2003018341

Contents

The Sun appears to be very large because it is much closer to Earth than other stars.

Sun Power

The Sun is a star like millions of others in the universe, with one important difference—Earth and the Sun are only 93 million miles (150 million kilometers) apart. Beyond the Sun, even our closest starry neighbors are so far off that their light appears only as pinpoints in the night sky.

Unlike Earth, the Sun is not a solid object. Instead, it is made up of a boiling mass of gases called hydrogen and helium, along with small amounts of other elements. Its center, or core, is the heaviest and hottest part of the Sun; at the star's surface is a much cooler layer.

The Sun's energy comes from deep within the core. Here, the scorching heat causes hydrogen atoms to

The gases that make up the Sun are so hot, they make the Sun glow.

move constantly. Some of the atoms slam together and stick, in a process called **nuclear fusion.**

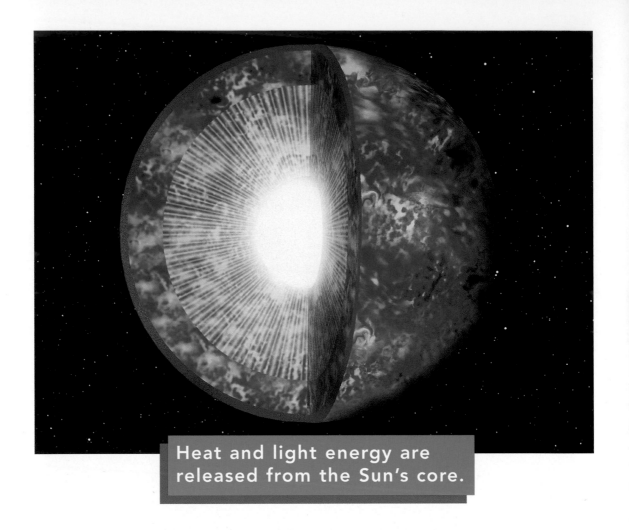

Heat and light energy are released from the Sun's core.

Fusion changes hydrogen into a heavier atom, helium. Along the way, energy is released as heat and light.

Energy created by fusion inside the Sun streams out into space in every direction. Light travels through space like waves on the ocean—but much faster. From the time light leaves the Sun, it takes just over eight minutes to reach Earth.

Earth absorbs only about one-billionth of the heat and light released by the Sun. Yet sunlight provides enough energy—called solar energy—

The Sun provides many living organisms on Earth with the energy to live, grow, and reproduce.

to warm our planet and support a wonderful variety of living things. Solar energy also provides a valuable supply of power that people can use to light and heat their homes, cook their food, and run appliances, such as refrigerators and computers.

Energy from the Sun can be collected and used in our homes.

The Life-Giving Sun

Life on Earth could not exist without the Sun. It warms the air, land, and water. The Sun controls the seasons and even the weather. Its light is the ultimate source of all our food.

It all begins with plants and tiny organisms called blue-green bacteria. Under a microscope, a

Plants on Earth use energy from the Sun to help make food. At right is a microscopic view of a plant leaf.

plant leaf or bacterial cell looks as though it's been decorated with green spots.

The bright color comes from **chlorophyll** molecules. These work like tiny factories, allowing the plant to make its own food. Just as an oven needs the power of electricity or natural gas to heat our meals, chlorophyll needs **fuel** before it can "cook." In this case the fuel is sunlight.

Light gives chlorophyll the energy to build nutritious sugar molecules from two simple ingredients, water and carbon dioxide. Some sugars

A rabbit munches on leaves and grass.

are used right away for growth and survival, while others are stored for later. Animals get their energy from the Sun indirectly, by eating plants or other animals.

A turtle soaks up the Sun's heat.

Many animals need sunlight for more than food, however. Imagine a turtle perched on a log on a clear spring morning. While the turtle may enjoy its quiet rest, sunbathing has a more important purpose.

Turtles and other reptiles are cold-blooded, meaning that their bodies do not stay at one constant, warm temperature. Soaking up the Sun's heat warms a reptile's blood, giving it the energy to move, hunt, and escape predators.

Like animals, humans have many uses for solar energy. Exposure to sunlight causes our skin to make vitamin D, which helps our bodies use calcium to build strong bones. Ancient people knew that

Campers roast marshmallows by the heat of a campfire.

wood, which grows because of sunlight, could be used to make fires. Today we still use many fuels that come from plants. Fossil fuels, such as oil, gas, and coal, formed millions of years ago from the decaying bodies of plants and animals.

Solar Food

When you sit down for your next meal, remember that solar energy made it possible. Tasty foods such as potatoes, carrots, and sunflower seeds are full of stored-up plant sugars. In addition, most of our meat comes from animals that ate plants. And while you're

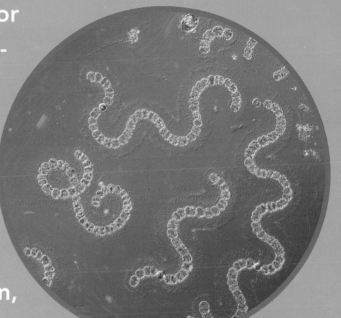

Blue-green bacteria live in water and make their own food.

not likely to make a meal of blue-green bacteria, these tiny organisms provide food for many animals. They are among the most common living things on earth, and also the oldest—blue-green bacteria have been using solar power to make their food for at least 3.5 billion years.

The Solar Home

Most homes need electricity and natural gas to make light, heat, and hot water. Solar homes collect the Sun's energy to meet many of these needs.

The first step in designing a solar home is to build with materials such as cellulose insulation, made from recycled

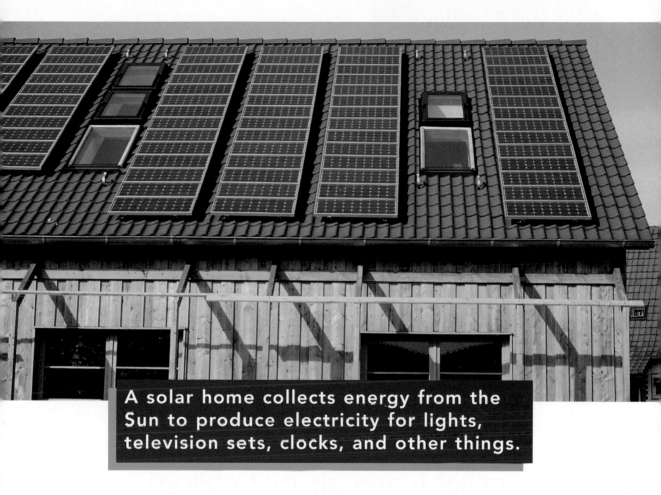

A solar home collects energy from the Sun to produce electricity for lights, television sets, clocks, and other things.

cardboard, which prevents heat from escaping through walls. Walls and floors can be built using stone, bricks, or

similar materials that absorb and hold heat well. This combination allows walls to release heat slowly, keeping rooms at a constant temperature.

In winter the Sun never gets high up in the sky—instead, it stays close to the southern horizon. A greenhouse-like room with glass walls and ceiling on

Rooms with glass walls trap heat inside.

the south side of the house allows winter sunlight to pour in but won't let heat escape through the solid glass. Warm air tends to rise, so ceiling fans can be installed to push heat into the rest of the house.

In summer the solar home's design helps reduce the need for air-conditioning. In summer, the Sun passes straight overhead, so the south side of the house gets very little direct sunlight. Window shades or curtains can be used to block

Closing the window shades helps keep the room cool.

light from entering the green-house in the early afternoon, when the Sun is high in the sky. High ceilings and ceiling fans help pull heat upward, out of the living space.

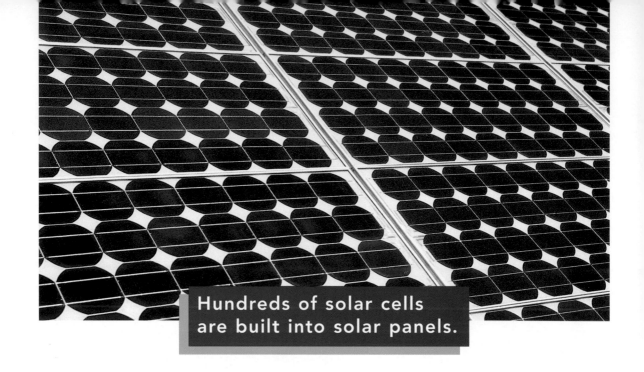

Hundreds of solar cells are built into solar panels.

Solar power can also be used to make electricity and hot water. Electricity is generated using **photovoltaic cells,** or solar cells, which are placed on rooftops. Each flat, round cell is made from silicon, a material found in sand. When silicon absorbs sunlight, the sunlight's energy causes a small electrical charge to move through the cell. Photovoltaic cells are wired to batteries that store the electricity. A couple of cells can be used to run a solar calculator or watch, while hundreds together can provide the electricity needed for a whole house.

Solar power can also be made using thin, rectangular boxes, called solar collectors, on rooftops. The box's lid is clear so sunlight can stream in,

These solar collectors use heat from the Sun to make hot water.

and its inside surface is painted black to absorb heat. Black piping snakes through the box. Water flows through the pipe, is heated by sunlight, then is pumped into a storage tank, where it stays hot for several days.

Ancient Solar Design

More than a thousand years ago, Anasazi Indians in the southwestern United States built their homes using solar design. The Southwest is one of the hottest regions in the United States, but it also gets snow in the winter. The Anasazi needed homes that protected them from the worst weather of both seasons. They placed their apartment-style houses in shallow caves high up on south-facing cliffs, which got the most winter sunlight. In summer the cliffs provided much-needed shade as the Sun rose high in the sky.

The Anasazi cliff houses were built to welcome the winter sunlight and be protected from the summer sunlight.

Electricity for Everyone

Since the 1950s, NASA has used panels of photovoltaic cells to power satellites in space, because sunlight is always available and the panels weigh far less than liquid fuels. Photovoltaic cells have even been used on cars and light

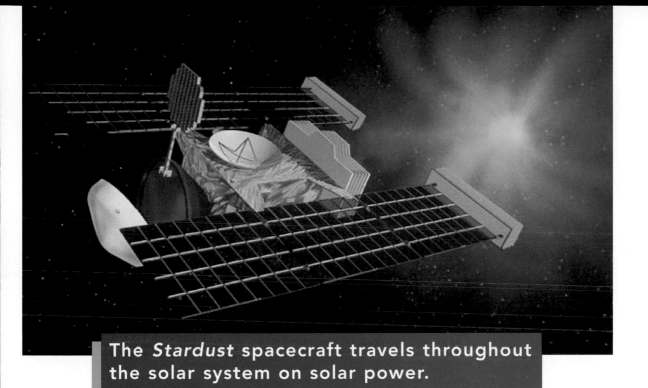

The *Stardust* spacecraft travels throughout the solar system on solar power.

planes. But much larger systems are needed to provide electrical power to industries or whole towns.

Deserts get direct sunlight throughout the year, and they are home to some of the largest

A solar power station in the desert

solar power stations in the world. Nine of the fourteen Solar Electric Generating Systems (SEGS) found in the United States are located in the sunny deserts of southern California. SEGS collect sunlight using trough collectors, bathtub-shaped panels that are lined with mirrors. The mirrors tilt to follow the Sun across the sky from east to west. Sunlight is focused onto an oil- or water-filled pipe that runs down the center of the

Curved mirrors concentrate the Sun's energy onto an oil- or water-filled pipe. Heat energy from the hot liquid is used to generate electricity.

trough. Inside the pipe, the fluid heats water, producing steam that pushes against the blades of a **turbine**. The turbine is attached to a **generator,** a round magnet surrounded by wires. The movement of the turbine causes the generator to spin, producing electricity.

Solar Two, also located in the California desert, is a solar power tower. It has a central tower more than 250 feet (76 meters) tall, surrounded by 1,800 flat, rectangular mirrors

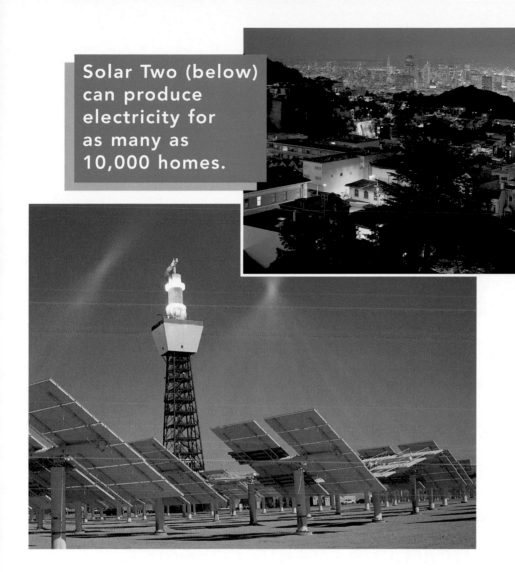

Solar Two (below) can produce electricity for as many as 10,000 homes.

called heliostats. The heliostats tilt, tracking the Sun's path and reflecting its light onto the tower.

At the top of the tower is a vat full of liquid salt, which boils under the Sun's reflected rays. Liquid salt holds heat better than oil or water, and may get as hot as 1,050° Fahrenheit (566° Celsius)—five times the temperature needed to boil water. This heat can then be stored and used later. Like the fluid in a trough collector, steam from the liquid salt is used to turn a generator to make electricity.

Energy for the Future

Today, more than three-quarters of all power used in the United States is produced from oil, natural gas, and coal. Oil and natural gas were discovered less than two hundred years ago, but they are already in danger- ously short supply. In just a thousand years we have mined

Oil and coal, which supply much of our power needs, are nonrenewable sources of energy.

much of our planet's ancient supply of coal. Experts believe we will begin to run out of these fossil fuels within two hundred years or less.

Fossil fuels are called **non-renewable resources** because they exist in limited amounts. They are being used up faster than they can be replaced, or renewed. That alone should encourage us to seek other sources of energy. But even if there were enough fossil fuels to last forever, there is another problem. When fossil fuels are burned to make energy,

Power plants such as the one above release harmful pollutants into nearby rivers and streams. Natural energy sources such as the stream at left can provide energy without causing pollution.

they release harmful gases that pollute our soil, air, and water.

The energy of sunlight, water, and wind can be harnessed

forever because they are constantly renewed and recycled in
nature. Yet less than 8 percent
of all the energy made in the
United States comes from these
renewable resources.

The problem lies in collecting
that energy. Solar power stations
take up a huge amount of space.
Because they can only make
power when the Sun is shining,
solar power plants must be built
in deserts or other sunny parts of
the world. Solar technology is
also very expensive.

Time and research can over-come some of these problems. For example, scientists are developing shiny plastic films that cost less to build than glass mirrors and are harder to scratch or break. Solar power stations can also be made to use a combination of fuels so they can work even when there is no sunlight—solar energy creating electricity by day and fossil fuels producing it at night.

No matter where the future leads us, we will always need

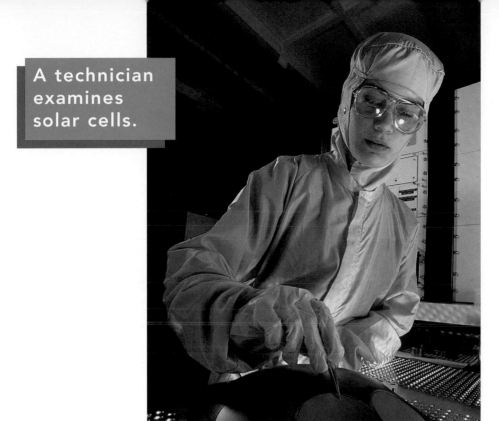

energy. Solar power may not be the easiest solution; but if we find more ways to harness the energy of the Sun, our future may be brighter than ever before.

To Find Out More

Here are some additional resources to help you learn more about solar power:

 **Books**

Gibson, Diane. **Solar Power.** Smart Apple Media, 2001.

Graham, Ian S. **Solar Power.** Raintree Steck-Vaughn, 1999.

Hewitt, Sally. **Full of Energy.** Children's Press, 1998.

Jones, Susan. **Solar Power of the Future: New Ways of Turning Sunlight into Energy.** Rosen Publishing, 2003.

Parker, Steve. **Fuels for the Future.** Raintree Steck-Vaughn, 1998.

Organizations and Online Sites

AstroForKids—The Sun
http://www.astronomy.com/content/static/AstroForKids/sun.asp

Look here to find background information on the Sun's size, structure, and temperature.

Solar Now, Inc.
http://www.solarnow.org/

Solar Now is an organization dedicated to educating people about renewable energy and the environment. Their site contains solar power information and activities for students and teachers, as well as a glossary of important terms.

Renewable Energy Resources from Earth Dog
http://www.earthdog.com/renew.html

This site has great background information on a variety of renewable energy sources, including solar, wind, and water power.

Energy Quest
http://www.energyquest.ca.gov/index.html

The California Energy Commission has compiled an exciting site just for students. Includes the "Energy Story" and "Science Projects." Meet scientists who study energy, and find a history of renewable energy.

Important Words

chlorophyll a green molecule found inside plants and blue-green bacteria that uses sunlight to make energy

fuel a source of energy that produces light, heat, or power

generator a machine in which steam is converted to electricity

nonrenewable resources materials that are formed by nature in limited amounts

nuclear fusion the process by which hydrogen atoms are joined inside the Sun to form helium

photovoltaic cells objects that convert sunlight into electricity

renewable resources water, wind, sunlight, and other materials that are naturally recycled or regrown

turbine a fan-shaped engine whose blades turn in response to the movement energy of steam, water, or wind

Index

Meet the Author

Christine Petersen is a middle school teacher who lives near Minneapolis, Minnesota. She has also worked as a biologist for the California Academy of Sciences, the U.S. Forest Service, the U.S. Geological Survey, and the Minnesota Department of Natural Resources, studying the natural history and behavior of North American bats. In her free time Christine enjoys snowshoeing, canoeing, bird watching, and writing about her favorite wild animals and wild places. She is a member of the Society of Children's Book Writers and Illustrators and is the coauthor of several previous True Books.